the skin you're in

True or False?

SURE IT'S *YOUR* BODY, BUT HOW MUCH DO YOU REALLY KNOW ABOUT TAKING CARE OF IT? TAKE THIS QUIZ TO TEST YOUR PERSONAL HEALTH IQ.

1 Feeling good about your body is vain.

2 Fats are bad. Healthy people don't eat them.

3 Aerobic exercise will sculpt your body.

4 Diets are the best way to lose weight.

5 Most teens don't get nearly enough sleep.

Answer key:

(1) False. Feeling good about your body is a key to self-confidence—and even happiness. But it isn't about being perfect (or being stuck up). Read more in Chapter One.

(2) False. Fats are necessary nutrients. But some fats are better for you than others. Read more in Chapter Two.

(3) False. Aerobic exercise is great for your heart. But it won't give you bulging biceps or six-pack abs. For that you need resistance training. Read more in Chapter Three.

(4) False. Diets can be a trap. Often people lose weight and then gain it back. Discover a better approach in Chapter Four.

(5) True. Most teens are totally sleep deprived! Find out why you need to catch those *z*'s in Chapter Five.

Photographs © 2008: Alamy Images: 100 (Ace Stock Limited), 70 (avatra images), 57 bottom (Yoav Levy/Phototake Inc.), 16 (Picture Partners), 77 (SW Productions/Photodisc); Corbis Images: 36 (Heide Benser/zefa), 68 (Jim Craigmyle), 60 top (Patrik Engquist/Etsa), 48 (Envision), 96 (Julie Fisher/zefa), 44 (Rick Gomez), 89 (Frithjof Hirdes/zefa), 86 (Jason Hosking/zefa), 57 top (image100), 84 (Lucidio Studio, Inc.), 20 (Maximilian Stock Ltd/PhotoCuisine), 58 top center (Steven Mark Needham/Envision), 5, 41 (Darius Ramazani/zefa), 58 bottom, 59 top (J. Riou/Photocuisine), 18 (Chuck Savage), 98 (SGO/Image Point FR), 59 top center (Dann Tardif/LWA), 6 (Frank Trapper), 58 top (Nation Wong/zefa); Getty Images: 91 (Tony Anderson), 92 (Lenora Gim), 47 (Sean Justice), 40 (Gen Nishino), 43 (Erin Patrice O'Brien), 60 bottom (Christina Peters), 59 bottom (Michael Rosenfeld), 82 (Donn Thompson); iStockphoto: 59 bottom center (Ron Bailey), 62 (Petko Danov); JupiterImages/Maximilian Stock Ltd./Food-Pix: 58 bottom center; Monty Stilson: cover; Photo Researchers, NY/Peter Gardiner: 28; PhotoEdit: 93 (Bill Aron), 52 (Mary Kate Denny), 27 (Susan Van Etten), 29 (Dana White), 79 (Colin Young-Wolff), 4, 15, 76, 80 (David Young-Wolff); Superstock, Inc./Creatas: 34; USDA: 30; VEER: 53 (Image Source Photography), 55 (Photodisc Photography).

Cover design: Marie O'Neill
Book production: The Design Lab
CHOICES editor: Bob Hugel

Library of Congress Cataloging-in-Publication Data
Webber, Diane, 1968–
The skin you're in: staying healthy inside and out / Diane Webber.
    p. cm.—(Scholastic choices)
Includes bibliographical references and index.
ISBN-13: 978-0-531-13869-4 (lib. bdg.)   978-0-531-20527-3 (pbk.)
ISBN-10: 0-531-13869-0 (lib. bdg.)   0-531-20527-4 (pbk.)
1. Teenagers—Health and hygiene—Juvenile literature. I. Title.
RA777.W378 2008
613'.0433—dc22   2007033347

©2008 Scholastic Inc.
All rights reserved. Published in 2008 by Franklin Watts, an imprint of Scholastic Inc. Published simultaneously in Canada. Printed in China. 62   SCHOLASTIC, FRANKLIN WATTS, and associated logos are trademarks and/or registered trademarks of Scholastic Inc.

5 6 7 8 9 10 R 18 17 16 15 14

SCHOLASTIC
CHOICES

Staying
healthy
inside
and out

the skin
you're in

Diane Webber

Franklin Watts®
AN IMPRINT OF SCHOLASTIC INC.
NEW YORK • TORONTO • LONDON • AUCKLAND • SYDNEY
MEXICO CITY • NEW DELHI • HONG KONG
DANBURY, CONNECTICUT

chapter five

68 Preventive Maintenance

How You Can Keep Yourself Looking, Feeling (and Smelling!) Good

There are lots of little things you can do to take care of the skin you're in. Our guide helps you get a handle on everything from acne to catching the right amount of *z*'s.

chapter six

86 The Big Pitfalls
Avoiding the Major Dangers of Teen Life

Sure, you already know that some of the biggest dangers teens face are drinking, smoking, and reckless driving. But brush up on this information anyway!

MORE INFORMATION

no body is perfect

no body
is perfect

LEARNING TO ACCEPT YOURSELF

Jamie-Lynn's Story

You don't get much luckier as a teen than Jamie-Lynn Sigler. The talented singer and actress played Meadow Soprano on the hit show *The Sopranos*. Surely she felt good about herself, right? Wrong! Sigler struggled with **anorexia nervosa**, a disease where a person starves oneself in a confused attempt for approval and perfection.

"During my junior year in high school, I was always a perfectionist," Jamie-Lynn told *Choices*. "I had a fear of failure. I was successful in many things. I had a career, I did well in school, and I had a great boyfriend. Then my boyfriend broke up with me, and school started getting harder, and my body started changing. It felt like everything was out of control. I started to question myself. Was I not pretty enough? Was I not thin enough?"

Jamie-Lynn started out just trying to lose 5 pounds (2 kilograms), but things snowballed: "Three months later, I was exercising almost five hours a day and eating next to nothing."

Today, things are very different for Jamie-Lynn. She realized that she had a big problem. She got therapy for her eating disorder, and she made a very important discovery. Self-acceptance—not perfection—is the key to health and happiness.

"Three months later, I was exercising almost five hours a day and eating next to nothing."

Accepting *This*??

Name five things that you wish you could change about your body. It's easy, right? According to a *U.S. News & World Report* survey on teen body image, fewer than half of boys and about a third of girls said they were happy with their bodies.

Now name five things that you love. Hmm, thinking . . . thinking . . . thinking. Much more difficult, right?

It is perfectly normal to not like things about your body. And it's even okay to want to improve yourself (in healthy, reasonable ways—and there are lots of suggestions in this book!). But there is one completely unchangeable fact about your body: you only get one. This is it for the long haul, the big journey, your whole life. Don't you think you should make peace with it?

Think of your body as a **LUXURY CAR**

Your body, and really your whole life, is going to work better, run more smoothly, and take you further if you take care of yourself. Think of your body as a luxury car. Appreciate it, enjoy it, and give it the fuel it needs and the attention it deserves.

REV
UP YOUR
SELF-ESTEEM

Want to feel better about yourself? Try these techniques:

1 Appreciate all that your body can do.

2 Make a list of ten things you like about yourself that are not related to your looks or weight.

3 Instead of focusing on body parts you don't like, look at yourself as a whole person.

4 Surround yourself with positive people.

5 Shut down the voices in your head that say negative things about your body.

6 Wear comfortable clothes that make you feel good about your body.

7 Do something nice for yourself.

8 Use the time that you might spend worrying about your body to do something to help others.

Source: National Eating Disorders Association

Try a "Fakeover"

Feeling down about yourself? Fake it. Stand up straight, smile, and tell yourself that you're great. Even if you don't believe it at first, pretending you're on top of the world can boost your confidence.

Changes, Changes, Changes

One of the things that threw Jamie-Lynn Sigler for a loop was puberty. The changes that happen as you morph from your kid self into your adult self are pretty dramatic. You might grow 5 inches (13 centimeters) in a single summer. Lots of guys suddenly start getting mistaken for their dads on the telephone, as their voices get deeper. And many girls are thrown off balance for a while by their new curves. Then there's the hair—in new places—that you have to learn to handle.

It's a lot to deal with at once. It's important to remember that these changes are happening (or will happen) to everyone else, too. Also keep in mind that everyone's biological clock is set a little differently. There is a wide range of "normal" for when girls will start their periods or when guys will grow a beard. Your timetable will probably be a lot like your biological mother's or father's (or your uncles' or aunts').

GROWTH SPURT
What's Average?

Most **GIRLS** reach their adult height between the ages of 12 and 19. The average age when girls reach their adult height is 15. And the average height for American women is 5'4" (163 cm).

Most **BOYS** reach their adult height between the ages of 14 and 18. The average age for boys to get close to their adult height is 16. But many guys continue to grow a bit more into their early 20s. The average height for American men is 5'9" (175 cm).

NIPS, TUCKS, TEENS
Young People and Plastic Surgery

Have you ever watched the TV shows *Extreme Makeover* or *Dr. 90210*? In these shows, people get plastic surgery to change their appearances. Is this a good idea for teens?

Experts disagree on the answer. Some say that plastic surgery is fine for mature teens who have done a lot of research and really understand what they are doing. Other experts worry that a desire to fix external flaws is covering up deeper problems inside. These critics think that many teens who really need counseling for their low self-esteem are turning to surgery instead.

In 2005, about 175,000 cosmetic surgeries were performed on people under age 18, according to the American Society for Aesthetic Plastic Surgery (ASAPS). Though some stories in the media suggest that plastic surgery has consistently increased among teens, ASAPS says this isn't true. According to ASAPS, there was actually a decline from 2004 to 2005.

The procedure teens have done more than any other? Rhinoplasty, also known as a nose job.

Reality Check

As you're dealing with the changes of puberty, it's natural to start comparing yourself to others. But be careful when those "others" are on the pages of magazines or on television. The media shows a twisted reality. Most people just don't look like that in real life. And even the celebrities themselves don't look that good all the time. Jamie-Lynn Sigler knows this from the inside. "I'm in the entertainment industry, and I know that a lot of the pictures you see in magazines aren't real," she says. "They are airbrushed. They are fake. If someone is really thin, they are sick."

On the other hand, it's not a bad idea to check out athletes and think about what it takes to get your body fit. Studies show that there is a strong connection between sports and positive body image. "Girls can look to athletes as alternative role models," says Leslie Heywood, author of *Pretty Good for a Girl: An Athlete's Story*. "Sports makes girls aware that there is a range of body types, and you don't have to fit one image."

Don't Go It Alone

The issues of self-acceptance, self-care, and self-love are not easy. They may seem simple ("Of course I love myself! What's not to love?"), but in fact, most of us are too critical of ourselves day in, day out. We're surrounded by media images that we don't measure up to. We remember insults a lot longer than compliments. And we have negative voices in our heads telling us we don't measure up.

It's really important to fight against all this critical input and to try to develop a positive self-image. That will help you form healthy bonds with others—and just make you generally happier.

the voice inside your head
Keep it positive!
Don't say anything to yourself that you wouldn't say to your best friend.

Look for support from sympathetic friends. And talk to the trusted adults in your life. Just talking about your feelings can make you feel better. You can also seek counseling, especially for serious issues such as depression, eating disorders, and drug or alcohol abuse.

The rest of this book is about taking care of yourself, so you can be on the positive cycle of thinking about yourself—not the negative one.

POSITIVE CYCLE

self-acceptance → positive self-talk → high self-esteem → taking care of self →

NEGATIVE CYCLE

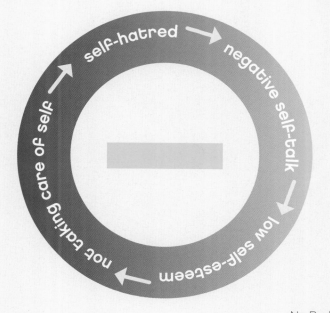

self-hatred → negative self-talk → low self-esteem → not taking care of self →

nutrition 411

nutrition 411

FOOD AS FUEL

Fuel Your Body

Let's keep thinking about our bodies as luxury cars. Great cars need premium gasoline, and the best fuel for our bodies is healthy, nutritious food. For cars, it's pretty simple: you just choose the best gas at the pump. But people are more complicated. To put the best fuel into your body, you have to fill up on knowledge first. That's what this chapter is all about.

Craig G. is a 12-year-old from Roslyn Heights, New York. His favorite meal is fajitas. He loves the way they come to your table at a restaurant, still sizzling, and he loves that you make each fajita yourself, adding what you like and leaving out what you don't. "I like sharing them, too," says Craig.

So anything that tastes that good must be bad for you, right? Actually, no. Craig can have a lot of

Would You Like Veggies With That?

Eating healthier means making smarter choices. Substitute good ingredients with great ones, and your fajita will be delicious and even more nutritious.

GOOD	GREAT
white flour tortilla	whole-wheat tortilla
grilled steak	grilled chicken
lots of white rice	some brown rice
some beans	lots of beans
a few vegetables	lots of vegetables
some sour cream	lots of salsa
lots of shredded cheese	a bit of shredded cheese

control over how healthy or unhealthy his meal is by the choices he makes. Check out the chart to the left to see how Craig can make his fajita healthier.

Both fajitas are delicious, but the one with "great choices" has fewer **calories**, less fat, more nutrients, and more **fiber**. It's premium fuel.

Here are the specifics:

Whole-wheat tortillas (or breads or cereals) are better for you than those made from white flour because whole grains have more fiber (which your digestive system needs) and more protein.

Grilled chicken has less of a bad kind of fat called saturated fat than grilled steak. It has fewer calories, too.

Rice is okay for you, but it's pretty high in calories. Don't eat too much. (Brown rice is healthier—and has more fiber—than white rice.)

Beans are a great combination of flavor, protein, and fiber.

Vegetables are super-low calorie and have lots of vitamins you can't get elsewhere. Load up!

Salsa has no fat. Sour cream has a lot. (But if you really love sour cream, have just a little.)

Cheese is also okay. It has calcium and protein—but also quite a bit of fat. Don't overdo it.

Do You Speak Nutrition?

Here are some terms you need to know.

Carbohydrates

They're also called carbs. They're an essential nutrient found in starchy foods like bread, cereals, potatoes, and corn. Fruits and vegetables are a combination of carbohydrates and fiber. Sweets contain lots of carbohydrates.

There are two kinds of carbs: simple and complex. Simple carbs are usually in white foods— white bread, potatoes, and sugar, for example. Your body breaks down simple carbs quickly and doesn't get a lot of nutrition from them.

Complex carbs are in foods like whole-grain bread, fruits, and vegetables. It takes more energy for your body to break these down, and you get more nutrition from them, too.

Calories

Calories are units of food energy. They are a measure of how much energy a certain food will give to your body. Your body will either burn off the calories you eat or store them in your fat cells.

Fat

Fat is the third essential nutrient. Another word for fats is lipids. Your body needs fats for healthy brain and nerve function, for healthy hair and skin, and for fighting off diseases. Olive oil, nuts, cheese, and fish are good sources of fat. You need small amounts of the right fats in a healthy diet. (See "Are Fats Good or Bad?" on page 24.)

Fiber

Fiber is the stuff in your food that your body doesn't digest, or break down chemically. But it still has an important role. Fiber keeps your digestive system running smoothly, and it makes you feel full when you eat. Fruits, vegetables, and beans all contain fiber.

Protein

Beef, chicken, pork, fish, eggs, soy, and beans all contain lots of protein, another essential nutrient. Protein is made up of **amino acids** that your body needs. Your body breaks down the amino acids in your food to build new cells.

ARE FATS
GOOD OR BAD?

Fats have a bad reputation and here's why:

1 gram of carbs = 4 calories
1 gram of protein = 4 calories
1 gram of fat = 9 calories

Fats have more than twice as many calories as carbs and protein. They are also denser. A slice of bread can have about 60 calories; so does less than a tablespoon of mayo. So it's pretty easy to make a turkey sandwich fattening by using mayonnaise.

Some types of fats are healthier than others. UNSATURATED FATS are the healthiest. OMEGA-3 FATTY ACIDS are one kind of unsaturated fat. They're found in fish and nuts and are good for your heart and your brain. MONOUNSATURATED FATS and POLYUNSATURATED FATS are also unsaturated fats. They're found mainly in plant sources such as olive oil, peanut oil, and canola oil. Some unsaturated fats seem to help protect people from heart disease.

SATURATED FATS come mainly from animal sources. Dairy and meat have saturated fat. Saturated fat isn't great for your heart, so you should eat lean meats and low-fat dairy products to limit the amount of saturated fat in your diet. Since these foods can be great sources of protein—another necessary nutrient—it's a good idea to limit saturated fats, rather than avoid them altogether.

TRANS-FATTY ACIDS, or trans fats, on the other hand, don't occur in nature and are very bad for your heart. They're created through a chemical process known as hydrogenation. This process makes foods last longer on the grocery store shelf without going bad. That's good for the profits of food companies (they make more money if things don't spoil). If you see "partially hydrogenated oil" on an ingredient list, you've got some trans fats.

SOURCES OF GOOD FATS:
walnuts, almonds, salmon, tuna, olive oil, canola oil
SOURCES OF BAD FATS:
margarine, lard, processed foods, animal products
THE BOTTOM LINE:
Eat small amounts of fat, and try to choose the good ones when you do.

Vitamins and Minerals

Vitamins and minerals are known as **micronutrients**. They're "micro" because you only need small amounts of them. We measure fats, carbs, and proteins in grams—they are macronutrients. (*Macro* means "big.") In contrast, vitamins and minerals are measured in milligrams, or 1/1000 of a gram.

Most vitamins are named by letters: vitamin A, B, C, D, and so on. Minerals include substances such as iron, zinc, and calcium. Some foods are fortified, or strengthened, with vitamins and minerals

(check out the side of your cereal box!), while others, such as green leafy veggies, are naturally rich in vitamins. Most doctors think it's best to get your vitamins by eating a variety of healthy foods. But if you don't, check with your doctor about taking a vitamin and mineral supplement.

Cholesterol

Cholesterol is a type of fat found mainly in animal tissue. It's carried in your bloodstream. Your body makes cholesterol; you also get cholesterol from the animal products you eat.

When you are an adult, your doctor will monitor your cholesterol. High cholesterol has been linked to heart disease. It can build up in your arteries, slowing the flow of blood. If it gets really bad, it can cause a heart attack.

The good news, though, is that there are two kinds of cholesterol. The good stuff is known as HDL (high-density lipoprotein). The bad stuff is LDL (low-density lipoprotein). Eating olive, peanut, and canola oils seems to boost good cholesterol and lower bad cholesterol.

Cholesterol can build up in your arteries.

Sodium

Sodium comes from salt (NaCl, as it's known in chemistry class). Most of the salt we eat comes from processed foods. (Processed foods are foods that are prepared in factories and are canned, boxed, or frozen before you purchase them.) Sodium, like fat, is another nutrient that your body absolutely needs—in limited quantities. The U.S. government recommends that you eat less than a teaspoon of salt a day.

Pyramid Power

Now you know the vocabulary of nutrition. But what should you actually eat? The U.S. Department of Agriculture (USDA) has an answer for that in the food pyramid. You'll find it at www.mypyramid.gov. The pyramid has a rainbow of vertical stripes, and it shows a figure running up the side. The idea is to emphasize the importance of eating a variety of foods—along with exercising (read more about exercise in the next chapter).

"The message we have in the . . . pyramid is that any positive change in the diet is wonderful," says Jackie Haven, a nutritionist with the USDA. "Small steps over time is a way to build a healthy diet."

Each stripe in the pyramid represents one of the five basic food groups. Moving from left to right, the largest stripe in the pyramid is for foods made from grains, such as bread, cereal, or pasta. Next comes the stripe for vegetables, then fruits. Then there is a skinny stripe, representing oils, a small, but essential part of your diet. The last two stripes on the pyramid are for dairy products and for foods rich in protein, such as meat, fish, and beans. For a healthful diet, you should eat foods from each group at every meal.

The different colored stripes in the pyramid boil down to one basic rule: "Make sure your plate has a lot of color on it, and that it comes from fruits and vegetables," says Susan Moores, a nutritionist and spokesperson for the American Dietetic Association.

"Small steps over time is a way to build a healthy diet."

YOUR DAY
in food

Here's the recommendation for what a 14-year-old boy who is 5'5" (165 cm), 115 pounds (52 kg), and gets 30 to 60 minutes of exercise a day should eat every day:

GRAINS: 8 ounces (227 grams), at least half of that being whole grains (good sources include oatmeal, whole-wheat bread, and popcorn)

VEGETABLES: 3 cups (720 milliliters), dark green and orange veggies are especially nutritious

FRUITS: 2 cups (480 mL), not including fruit juice, which is all sugar and no fiber

MILK: 3 cups (720 mL), including yogurt, cheese, and cottage cheese

MEAT AND BEANS: 6.5 ounces (184 g), beans and lean cuts of meat are best

OILS: 7 teaspoons, vegetable oils such as olive oil and canola oil are best

The pyramid also has different suggestions based on your age, gender, height, weight, and activity level. You can go to the Web site, put in the facts about YOU, and then get personalized food recommendations.

The tiniest sliver of the pyramid is the yellow band, representing oils and extras such as sugars and fats. Our hypothetical teen should aim to get 7 teaspoons of oils a day and shouldn't eat more than 360 calories in sugary, fatty foods. But that is enough to have a cup of ice cream at the end of the day!

fast-lane foods

Fast food is a fact of life for most teens. Here are some strategies for keeping it as healthy as it is tasty and fun.

DOWNSIZE: Instead of a triple burger and large fries, order a kid's meal. It tastes just as good, and the portion sizes are healthier. Plus, you get a toy for your kid brother.

GO GREEN: Most fast-food joints offer tasty salads these days. Choose the low-fat dressings and grilled chicken toppings.

BE PICKY: Some restaurants have more healthy menu choices than others. Wendy's chili and baked potato are good calls. And at Subway, you can order sandwiches with lots of veggies and low-fat meats on whole-grain fresh bread.

PIZZA POWER: If you order a thin crust with a veggie topping (no extra cheese), then a slice or two of pizza can be good for you.

move
it

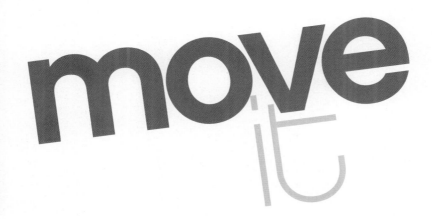

move it

EXERCISE YOUR OPTIONS

The Key to Getting Going

Let's go back to that idea of your body as a luxury car. What would be the point of having a great car that stayed in the garage all day? Not only is it kind of sad, but it would be bad for the car.

Cars are meant to be driven and your body is meant to move. The key to getting yourself going (and going and going—you need to do it every day!) is to find something you love to do.

For Christopher W., that "something" is swimming. The 16-year-old from Somerdale, New Jersey, fell in love with swimming early on because his grandmother had a pool. "I started out with swim lessons at the Y," he says. "And then I would just spend hours every day in the summer in grandmom's pool until I could swim like a fish." What started as summer fun when he was a little kid has become a great way to stay fit. "Swimming exercises every muscle in your body," says Christopher, who got his lifeguard certification last summer. "It's had a huge impact on me."

Think back to when you were a little kid. What did you love to do for active play? That might give you a clue about an exercise that you wouldn't dread doing now.

TURNING
PLAY
INTO
exercise

then   now

then	now
playing tag with friends →	**cross-country, field hockey, lacrosse, track, jogging**
splashing in a kiddie pool →	**swim team, diving, swimming laps**
dancing to music videos →	**dance classes, aerobics classes, exercise DVDs**
playing kickball →	**football, soccer, basketball, volleyball**
riding a tricycle →	**skateboarding, bike riding**

FIND YOUR
Favorite Exercise

Answer these questions for yourself. Then read the key for some suggestions of exercises that might fit your lifestyle.

1

MY FAVORITE PLACE TO BE IS:

a. outside. I love nature.
b. inside. I love my air conditioning.
c. wherever my friends are.

2

I LOVE TO GO FAST.

a. true
b. false

3

IN MY LIFE, MUSIC IS:

a. absolutely essential.
b. optional.

4

MY SCHEDULE IS:

a. completely packed. I'm always busy.
b. pretty open. I have lots of downtime.

1

If you answered:

(a) Jogging, biking, and hiking are some great outdoor options.

(b) Working out at a gym on treadmills and weight machines might be for you.

(c) Go for team sports or group exercise classes. Even activities like jogging can be done with a pal. But remember: the point of exercise is to break a sweat!

2

If you answered TRUE, you have a need for speed. Try bike riding, in-line skating, or skateboarding.

3

If you answered:

(a) Try to incorporate music in your workout. Listen to music while you run or just dance around your room.

(b) You still might want to try exercising to music. Studies show that music energizes exercisers and helps them work harder without noticing.

4

If you answered:

(a) Get creative about squeezing activity into your busy life. Park far away in parking lots to get some extra walking. Take the stairs instead of elevators. And make the most of gym class. It might be your only shot all day at getting active.

(b) Be sure to schedule some active time every day. Walking, jogging, or shooting baskets all count.

"Do I Really Have to Exercise?"

The short answer is yes. You really, really do have to exercise. You don't have to dominate your gym class, but you do need to find something active to do. You've got to take that luxury car body of yours for a spin every day.

Most people think they know the most obvious benefit of exercise: you look better. Fit bodies are attractive, yes. But the benefits of exercise go beyond looks. In fact, some people with thin bodies just lucked out. If a thin person doesn't exercise, he or she is less fit than a person who is heavier and works out every day.

There's another problem with looks being your major motivator for exercising. You can't get toned overnight. You won't look totally buff the day after you start working out. You might see results six weeks later. It's hard to wait that long, so don't get discouraged before you get there.

Fortunately, there are some benefits of exercise that you can see immediately. If you work out doing something you love today, here's what you may IMMEDIATELY notice:

- you'll have more energy;
- you'll be in a better mood;
- you'll sleep better;
- you'll feel less stressed out;
- you'll feel better about yourself.

Those are just the short-term benefits of exercising. Over the long term, exercising as a teen will build bones strong enough to last your entire life. If you make exercise a lifelong habit, you'll be at a lower risk for heart disease, stroke, various cancers, depression, and type 2 diabetes (which is a growing problem for teens; read more about it in the next chapter).

Still Not Convinced?

If you hate to exercise, you aren't alone. Unfortunately, many teens are not getting the exercise they need. According to a 2007 study, the average girl barely exercises outside of gym class when she hits her late teens. Researchers at the National Heart, Lung, and Blood Institute tracked nearly 2,400 girls over a nine-year period beginning at age 9 or 10, from the Washington, D.C.; Cincinnati, Ohio; and Richmond, California, areas. After estimating the amount of energy the girls burned in after-school activities, they saw that the girls' overall activity scores plunged by 83 percent by the study's end.

And here's where this trend leads: lack of activity can lead to weight gain. Weight gain can lead to low self-esteem. Low self-esteem can lead to depression and more weight gain. It is another one of those no-fun cycles that are hard to break. Check out the box to the right for some ideas on how to break the cycle with exercise that doesn't feel like exercise.

Lack of activity can lead to weight gain.

Shh!
don't call it
EXERCISE!

Slip these activities into your daily life, and you'll hardly notice yourself getting fit.

CLIMB THE STAIRS. Skip the elevator or escalator and take the stairs instead. Even if you only walk up one flight of steps, you'll burn calories and tone your muscles. And walking downstairs is great exercise, too.

PARK THE CAR. Do you live close enough to your destination to walk or ride a bike? Use your legs to get there and leave your car in the garage. Or ask your mom to park (or drop you off) in a faraway spot at the mall.

GO SHOPPING. Take a lap or two around the mall before you hit the shops. And try to avoid the food court!

WATCH TV. As you're watching your favorite sitcom, do some cardio (march in place, jog, jump rope) while the show is on, and some resistance work (sit-ups, push-ups, chair dips) while the commercials are on. By the time the show is over, you'll have done a complete workout.

DO YOUR CHORES. Earn points at home and burn calories at the same time. Shoveling snow, mowing the lawn, raking, walking the dog, and vacuuming are all great forms of exercise.

Cardio Versus Weight Training

Do you know the two main types of exercise?
Cardiovascular exercise (also known as aerobic exercise and stamina training) is continuous movement—such as walking, jogging, or biking—that increases your heart rate. *Cardio* means "heart."

Weight training (also called **resistance training** and strength training) is exercise that builds your skeletal muscles. (Those are the muscles that move your limbs and support your torso.) Weight training involves lifting weights or using the weight of your own body for resistance (this is what you're doing when you do push-ups, pull-ups, or sit-ups). Proper form in weight training is much more important than trying to lift the heaviest weight possible.

Which form of exercise is better for you? In the past, experts went back and forth on this question. In the 1980s, aerobic exercise was super popular. Aerobic activities burn more calories than weight lifting, so it seemed like that was all you needed.

Today, experts say that being aerobically fit is extremely important, but it's not enough. Weight training builds your muscles, and bigger muscles need more fuel. This means that you will burn more calories throughout your day. Weight training in young adulthood also strengthens your bones, a benefit that lasts for years. And a recent review of childhood **obesity** studies showed that kids who combined strength training and aerobic exercise had the greatest weight loss.

There is one important difference between cardio training and weight training. Experts say you should do some cardio every day. A 30-minute walk every day is great. But your muscles need time to recover after strength training. So you can either do your resistance routine every other day, or work just your upper body one day and your lower body the next.

Play It Safe

Another important category of exercise is stretching. Stretching your muscles keeps you **flexible** and helps you avoid injury during a workout. It also improves your circulation, relaxes you, and helps your muscles recover faster. You shouldn't stretch a cold muscle. You should warm up first by walking or marching in place. It is even more beneficial to stretch as part of your cooldown, during the last five minutes of your workout. Don't be surprised if you can stretch farther than when you started. The best technique is to hold each stretch for 30 to 60 seconds. (But don't bounce; that can lead to injury.)

Here are some other tips for staying safe when you're working out:

DRINK UP: Always drink plenty of water before, during, and after an activity to prevent dehydration. Drink before you feel thirsty.

SHELL OUT FOR SHOES: Buy running shoes for running, basketball shoes for basketball, etc. The right shoes cushion and support your feet to absorb the shocks of a particular sport. That can mean the difference between playing comfortably and sitting out with foot or ankle problems. Replace worn-out shoes, too.

RESPECT PAIN: Strenuous exercise can—and probably will—cause soreness from using new groups of muscles. But persistent pain is different. It's your body's way of saying you've got an injury. Take it as a signal to stop an activity until the injury has healed.

SWEAT THE SMALL STUFF: Treat even minor injuries properly. Don't resume activity until an injury has healed completely, or you may face bigger problems down the line.

KEEP YOUR TEETH: If you play collision sports such as hockey, football, or rugby, wear a mouth guard. Some trainers recommend mouth guards for any sport involving physical contact.

ASK QUESTIONS: If you're unsure about how, when, or where you should exercise, ask a gym teacher, coach, doctor, or parent. Or check one of the many books or Web sites on virtually every kind of athletic activity from archery to yoga. Some good places to start can be found in Further Resources on page 106.

managing your weight

managing your weight

AND MANAGING THE WEIGHT ISSUE

Overweight Teens

The statistics are harsh. Since 1980, the number of teenagers and kids who are dangerously overweight or obese has more than doubled. Today, 15 percent of kids ages 6 to 18 are overweight, according to a report from the Federal Interagency Forum on Child and Family Statistics.

At age 13, Christianne of Merrick, New York, was one of the statistics. She stood 5'6" tall (168 cm) and weighed 180 pounds (82 kg). She'd had back surgery two years before and become inactive. But she didn't realize how much weight she'd gained until one day when she was shopping for jeans. The size 12 didn't fit, and Christianne was very upset. "I had an emotional breakdown in the store," she said. "I started crying, and I couldn't stop."

Christianne began to try to lose weight, but she had limited success. It was very hard to stay on track, eating small portions of the right foods. She had a big turnaround the summer she was 15, when she went to a weight-loss camp and lost 25 pounds (11 kg). "I had felt like I could do it alone, but I couldn't," she says. "I needed someone standing over me telling me that I couldn't have another slice of cake."

Christianne followed up camp by getting involved with team sports at her school. Today, she is lighter, healthier, and feeling much better about herself. Her advice to overweight teens: "Lose weight for yourself, not for someone else. I tried to change for other people and I wasn't happy. When I did it for myself, it made it so much easier."

do you really need to
LOSE WEIGHT?

Who is overweight and who isn't? These days, experts answer that question with a ratio called the body mass index (BMI). This formula takes your height and weight into account. Here's how you calculate it. Then go to the next page to find out what these numbers mean.

$$\frac{\text{(weight in pounds)}}{\text{(height in inches x height in inches)}} \times 703 = \boxed{\textbf{BMI}}$$

The metric system is a little easier.

$$\frac{\text{(weight in kilograms)}}{\text{(height in meters x height in meters)}} = \boxed{\textbf{BMI}}$$

If your calculator batteries aren't working, you could also go to www.nhlbisupport.com/bmi for an online BMI calculator.

So, Christianne's BMI when she was 13 was:

$$\frac{180}{66 \times 66} \times 703 = \boxed{\textbf{29.0}}$$

BMI
CATEGORIES

underweight = less than 18.5

normal weight = 18.5–24.9

overweight = 25–29.9

obese = 30 or greater

So, with a BMI of 29, Christianne was near the top of the overweight category. Her range for the normal weight category is between 115 and 154 pounds (52 and 70 kg). This is a very wide range, and it includes people who have small frames, as well as people who are more solidly built.

Weighty Problems

Why should we care that more teens are overweight today? On a personal level, anyone who has struggled with a weight problem knows it can be emotionally difficult. Other kids can be cruel, and being teased doesn't feel good.

But the dangers of being seriously overweight or obese go beyond emotional issues. Obesity is a very serious health risk. Dr. William Dietz, director of the Centers for Disease Control and Prevention's Division of Nutrition and Physical Activity, calls the problem of overweight kids "the most significant nutritional problem in the United States today."

Obesity increases your chances of developing asthma, heart disease, and—most dangerous for kids—**diabetes**. Diabetes results when the body can't properly regulate its blood-sugar level.

"[Childhood obesity is] the most significant nutritional problem in the United States today."

blood SUGAR

Time out for some background information on blood sugar. Your body breaks down the food you eat into glucose, a kind of sugar. Your blood then carries this glucose to all your cells and gives them energy.

It's important that the amount of glucose in your blood not be too low or too high. Ordinarily, those levels are controlled by substances called enzymes. But in people with diabetes, these enzymes don't work properly, and blood sugar is too high.

Diabetes comes in two types. Type 1 is not linked to obesity, but type 2 often is. Ten years ago, type 2 diabetes was almost unknown in children and adolescents. Today, it accounts for nearly half of new cases of childhood diabetes in some communities. The damage diabetes causes in young people happens slowly, but it is irreversible. Teens with diabetes are at a high risk for developing serious complications as adults.

What kinds of complications? "Diabetes is the number-one cause of blindness, the number-one cause of kidney failure, and the number-one cause of loss of limb other than car accidents," says Dr. Henry

Anhalt, co-director of Kids Weight Down, a program for overweight teenagers in Brooklyn, New York.

Still, being overweight doesn't mean you'll get diabetes. Thin people sometimes get it, too. The disease can also be inherited, passed down between generations. Kids who have a parent or other relative with type 2 diabetes have a higher risk of developing the disease, especially if they become overweight.

If you have any of these additional risk factors, it's even more important to try to keep your weight down.

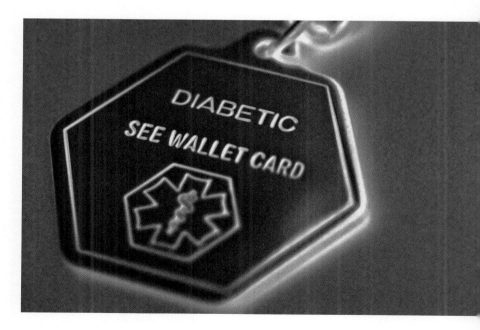

"IT'S NOT YOUR FAULT"

Why is the obesity **epidemic** happening? Experts agree that there are a lot of cultural changes causing people to gain weight. Obesity isn't limited to young people, but the deck is really stacked against teens.

"When overweight kids walk into my office, the first thing I tell them is, 'It's not your fault,'" says Dr. Henry Anhalt, of Kids Weight Down. "They start to cry. After years of hearing negative things from their peers, their parents, and sometimes even their physicians, it's a major relief for the kids."

See a few of the causes of the obesity epidemic in the column to the right.

Foods that are marketed to teens tend to be high in calories and fat. They are also usually served in huge portions.

Many schools have eliminated or cut back on recess and physical education classes.

Fewer kids can walk or bike to school than did in the past. Many parents aren't comfortable allowing their kids to wander around the neighborhood on bikes or on foot.

Popular pastimes, such as playing video games or surfing the Internet, are sedentary, meaning you sit to do them. So teens aren't getting enough exercise.

Losing It

If you do need to lose some weight, you are most definitely not alone. What is the best approach to take? Should you go on a diet?

Believe it or not, the answer is no. You probably do need to reexamine your food choices. And you probably do need to find ways to get more active. But the problem with the word *diet* is that a diet is something you go on, and then you go off. Lots of people lose weight on diets, but the vast majority of them gain it all back—and then some.

The better way to think about losing weight is to start replacing bad habits with good ones. These are habits that can serve you well for a lifetime— keeping that luxury-car body of yours running well and looking good, too.

Ten Good Habits

Here are ten good habits that will help you shed pounds or just become healthier—and stay that way.

1. Eat breakfast. Fueling your body in the morning will get you burning more calories all day. The ideal breakfast includes some protein and a bit of fat. Cereal with low-fat milk and fruit is a great breakfast.

2. Plan snacks. Have a midmorning and a midafternoon snack, so you never let yourself get famished (that's when overeating happens). Try yogurt with fruit, or peanut butter on whole-grain crackers. Limit your portion size to what the label says a portion is.

3. Eat your fruits and veggies. If you only do one new thing, do this one! We won't bore you with the vitamins-and-nutrients-are-so-good-for-you yadda yadda you've been hearing it since you were little. Here's why you should eat them if you need to lose weight: They fill you up. They can also be savory. Or sweet. Or tangy. Fresh is best. But frozen, jarred, or canned is better than nothing.

4. Drink water. Every cell in your body needs it. And it fills you up, too. The amount of water each person needs varies, but choosing water over drinks that contain sugar is a great way to save calories.

5. Choose lean protein and low-fat dairy.

Fish, chicken, turkey, eggs, and lean beef are good choices. A 3-ounce (85-g) serving is about the size of a deck of cards. Milk that has 1 percent or 2 percent milk fat is delicious. So are the cheeses made from this milk. Give nonfat milk and cheese a try—you'll save even more calories.

6. Keep track.

Writing down what you've eaten in a journal or keeping track of it online (try mypyramidtracker.gov) is another strategy that studies have shown helps people lose weight.

7. Measure your food.

Get some measuring cups and use them to control your portion sizes. One cup of pasta is a reasonable portion. One-half cup of frozen yogurt is a good dessert. (For more advice on portion sizes go to www.kidshealth.org/teen/food_fitness/dieting/portion_size.html.)

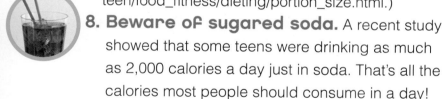

8. Beware of sugared soda.

A recent study showed that some teens were drinking as much as 2,000 calories a day just in soda. That's all the calories most people should consume in a day! One 12-ounce can of cola has 150 calories and absolutely no nutritional value. If you drank a six-pack, that would be about half the total calories you should have in a day. And watch out for fruit juices. They are high in calories as well. Drink diet soda—or even better, water!

9. **Make your salad bowl large and your ice cream bowl small.** A 2006 study showed that the bigger a bowl someone was given, the larger a portion of ice cream the person scooped. Get yourself a small bowl for treats. And find a really, really big bowl to make your salads in! This is a way to control your portions without giving it too much thought.

10. **Treat yourself.** One of the reasons diets often fail is that dieters feel deprived. When they slip and have a forbidden food, they feel like it's a lost cause and give up all their good habits. Avoid this by planning your treats. Maybe you can have one-half cup of fat-free chocolate pudding every night. Or maybe every Saturday you treat yourself to the foods you love. You might have to eat them in moderation or find lower-calorie versions of them. But don't make the mistake of thinking you can never eat your favorite foods again. You just have to control how much of those foods you eat!

SMART
substitutions

When you get a snack attack for something in the left-hand column, satisfy the craving with one of the lower-calorie options on the right.

If you love	Instead try
ice cream	→ light ice cream, frozen yogurt
potato chips	→ baked chips, low-fat popcorn
chocolate	→ fat-free chocolate pudding
soda	→ flavored seltzer
chips and salsa	→ baby carrots and salsa
melted cheese sauce	→ reduced-fat shredded cheese

IF YOU MUST HAVE
a candy bar . . .

Even in the junk-food aisle, some choices are better than others. A Snickers bar has 273 calories. A 3 Musketeers bar has 96 calories. You could also satisfy a craving for chocolate with a chocolate-flavored protein bar. These have 150 to 200 calories but are also packed with protein, fiber, and vitamins.

what NOT to do

Here are three weight-loss moves that are really bad ideas.

NOT EATING ALL DAY

You skip breakfast, then lunch. By afternoon you're starving, but you tell yourself you'll hold off a little longer and eat a small dinner. But it almost never works that way.

"I wouldn't eat much during the day, and then I'd eat a lot at night," says teen Shanisha in the book *Weight Loss Confidential*. Shanisha says she could "eat five bags of chips in three minutes." Another teen in the book also tried fasting but said, "It made me feel sick and useless."

These results are typical of this bad strategy. "Kids just can't lose weight this way," says Anne Chasson, a nutritionist from Palo Alto, California. "In fact, they wind up gaining weight because as soon as they get home, they gorge on everything in sight."

She's not talking carrot sticks. Those hunger pangs usually send you straight to high-calorie junk like candy, chips, and soda. You can end up eating hundreds or even thousands more calories than if you'd eaten healthy meals throughout the day.

Eating poorly messes with your head, too. "When kids overeat like this, they wind up depressed, and their self-esteem takes a nose dive," says Chasson. You tell yourself, "Oh no, I've blown it," and you feel unattractive and unlovable. So what do you do? You do it all over the next day—both to punish yourself and to blot out the bad feelings.

HIGH-PROTEIN/LOW-CARB DIET On this diet, you severely limit high-carbohydrate foods such as bread, pasta, cereal, potatoes, sweets, and fruit juice. You can eat all the meat, eggs, cream, and other fats you want. The idea is that without carbohydrates to use as fuel, your body uses stored fat—and you lose weight.

However, weird things start happening to your body when it's deprived of glucose, the fuel it makes from carb-rich foods. Without carbs, your body makes fuel from fat. That fuel is called ketones. Ketones are nasty. They give you bad breath, make you feel dizzy, and some research shows they may cause acid buildup in the bloodstream—which can be lethal.

Why do millions of Americans suffer through this diet? It's because on the diet, you can lose lots of weight in the first few weeks. But it's water weight, not fat. The weight returns as soon as you start eating carbs again. And you will! Even meat lovers start craving bagels, pasta, and other carbs after being deprived.

David, interviewed in *Weight Loss Confidential*, learned this the hard way. "I looked at my failures from the past, like the Atkins diet [a popular low-carb diet], and realized that as soon as I went off the diet, the weight came back on." David turned that around and succeeded when he started "taking little steps" that he could live with forever, such as giving up soda and unhealthy snacks.

PILL POPPING Ephedrine makes you burn extra calories and suppresses your appetite. There's just one downside: It can kill you. Ephedrine or Ma Huang (an ephedrine-containing herb) can be found in the diet aisle of most health-food stores. Though it may look safe, at least 60 people in the last seven years have died after taking ephedrine. Some of them were teens.

Hundreds of others have suffered heart attacks, strokes, or seizures, or have attempted suicide after taking the drug. Why? Ephedrine can overstimulate the heart and nervous system, especially in people prone to problems with the heart or nervous system. Don't take it!

Other diet pills—like Dexatrim and Acutrim—may be just as dangerous. In 2000, the Food and Drug Administration recommended that phenylpropanolamine, an ingredient in every over-the-counter appetite suppressant, be banned because it increases the risk of stroke in young women up to 15 times.

Need another reason to skip diet pills? They don't work unless you eat less or exercise more, and any weight you lose almost always comes back when you stop taking the pills. Want more proof? In the book *Weight Loss Confidential*, author Anne M. Fletcher contacted 104 teens and preteens who had successfully lost weight and kept it off. One hundred and one of them did not use diet pills.

DECODING
the label

By law, every prepared food has a label like this one. It contains important information that you can use when making decisions about what to eat.

SERVINGS: Pay attention to how many servings are in the container. The information on the label is for one serving, not necessarily the whole container.

FAT: When looking at the total amount of fat, pay attention to what kind of fat is in the food. Though this yogurt contains 5 percent of your daily total fat, it has 10 percent of your saturated fat.

Nutrition Facts
Serving Size 1 Cup (8 fl oz) (245.0g)
Servings Per Container 1

Amount Per Serving

Calories 208   Calories from Fat 28

                         % Daily Value*

Total Fat 3.1g	5%
Saturated Fat 2.0g	10%
Polyunsaturated Fat 0.1g	
Monounsaturated Fat 0.8g	
Cholesterol 12mg	4%
Sodium 162mg	7%
Total Carbohydrates 33.8g	11%
Fiber 0.0g	0%
Sugars 33.8g	
Protein 12.1g	

Vitamin A 2%	•	Vitamin C 3%
Calcium 42%	•	Iron 1%

* Based on a 2000 calorie diet

CARBOHYDRATES: The amount of total carbohydrates is fiber plus sugars. Look at how much of the total carbohydrates are fiber. This yogurt is not a good source of fiber.

PROTEIN: This yogurt is an excellent source of protein. A percentage is not given because it varies greatly depending on age, gender, and activity level.

WHAT WORKS?
activity!

Studies have shown that there is one big difference between people who keep off lost weight and those who gain it back. The difference is regular exercise. So get moving!

Healthy Helpers

If you want to make a commitment to lose weight, it helps to have a team pulling for you. Start with your family. Let the person who does the grocery shopping know that you want to make healthier food choices. Give them a list (don't forget the fruits and veggies!)—or better yet, tag along and read the labels as you go. (But never do your food shopping when you're hungry. It can be harder to make smart choices when your stomach is doing the thinking.)

You can also explore finding a weight-loss community online. These sites can be good ongoing sources of support. (Just remember never to reveal your full name or other personal information online.)

SparkPeople.com is one free site devoted to helping people get the information and support they need to lose weight. Another helpful Web site is mypyramidtracker.gov. On this site, you can record what you eat and your activity each day. You can see whether you are meeting the government's recommendations for a healthy diet or not.

Losing weight is not easy, but neither is being overweight. Think of healthy food habits and activity as an investment in yourself. You are worth it!

preventive maintenance

preventive maintenance

HOW YOU CAN KEEP YOURSELF LOOKING, FEELING (AND SMELLING!) GOOD

The Importance of Upkeep

The luxury car in the garage needs to be tuned up and washed occasionally. And guess what? So do you. This chapter is about some other things you can do to keep yourself in good shape.

Get Your Z's

On a typical night in the summer, Matthew M. of Baton Rouge, Louisiana, falls asleep some time between midnight and 2 A.M. "Most of the time I'll just stay up in bed and think too much," says Matthew, who is 16. "I have to wake up at 10 A.M. no matter what. My parents won't allow me to stay in bed any later. I average seven or eight hours a night." During the school year, his routine is to go to sleep at around 10 or 11 P.M. "But I have to wake up at 5:30. That's early!" he says. If he doesn't get at least seven or eight hours of sleep, he feels it: "I'm more irritable, more cranky than usual in the morning."

Matthew is among the 80 percent of teens who don't get enough sleep, according to the National Sleep Foundation. Experts agree that teens need about nine and a half hours of sleep, but most average just over seven. And many get by on much less. "I think most teens don't even know what it's like to be fully awake," says Dr. Mary Carskadon, a sleep researcher at Brown University. "It's like they are walking around with bad eyesight. When you get them back on a healthy sleep schedule, they are shocked at how clear everything is—and how good they feel."

Your brain needs sleep, and not getting enough disrupts your ability to concentrate. Lack of sleep can also lower your immune system defenses. Being sleep deprived puts you at risk for all kinds of problems, including car crashes, colds, depression, diabetes, and obesity.

Here are some tips for getting a better night's sleep:

BE CONSISTENT. Have a regular bedtime, and don't stray from it more than two nights in a row.

DON'T MESS UP YOUR SLEEP SCHEDULE ON THE WEEKENDS. Don't stay up more than one hour later on the weekends, and don't sleep more than three hours later than usual.

RELAX. Do something calming and relaxing right before bed. Avoid bright light and energetic exercise (but remember that exercising earlier in the day will help you sleep at night).

START BRIGHT. Get into bright light as soon as possible in the morning. This will get your brain ready to start the day.

a LATE start

Research has shown that the natural sleep cycle for teens runs from about midnight to 9 A.M. But middle schools and high schools often have start times much earlier than that. No wonder so many people nod off in first period! Times are changing, though. So far, individual schools or districts in 19 states have pushed back their start times. More than 100 school districts in an additional 17 states are considering doing the same thing.

Dodging Illness

How can you stay as healthy as possible? If you've read this far, you probably have a few ideas about how to answer that. Eat healthy foods, get active, and get enough sleep are three good answers. All three of these things have an added benefit: They help your body fight off minor illnesses like colds and the flu.

Your body is constantly engaged in a war against the germs that can make you sick. Your skin protects you from these germs. So do your nose, throat, and respiratory system. And the germs that get through these front-line defenses are usually killed by your white blood cells.

Here are some more things you can do to help your body fight the good fight.

WASH YOUR HANDS. Germs travel from person to person through touch. So wash your hands throughout the day. Make sure you lather with soap for at least 15 seconds.

DON'T SMOKE. Smoking weakens your respiratory system, making it less able to fight off illness.

DRINK FLUIDS. Doctors believe that drinking plenty of water helps keep the body hydrated and functioning properly.

LIMIT STRESS. You're twice as likely to catch a cold when your emotions are out of whack. When you're stressed, breathe deeply to calm yourself and remove yourself from the stressful situation, if possible.

LAUGH IT UP. Studies have shown that laughter can relieve stress and boost your body's production of disease-fighting T cells.

CONSIDER VITAMINS. Vitamins and supplements can boost your body's immune system, giving it added ability to fight off infections. Ask your doctor about the possible benefits of vitamin C and other vitamins and supplements.

CHANGE YOUR TOOTHBRUSH. Toothbrushes are a surefire way to transfer germs into your body. Change your toothbrush every couple of months, even when you're healthy. Always buy a new one after recovering from a cold or the flu.

GET A FLU SHOT. Flu shots are often recommended for people who spend lots of time in crowded places (such as classrooms and dorms), as well as for people with certain health conditions such as asthma and diabetes.

Sneezing 101

You know everything you need to know about sneezing, right? Well, maybe not. Did you know that:

YOU SHOULDN'T HOLD IN A SNEEZE. "You can definitely hurt yourself by holding in a sneeze," says Dr. Lisa Harris, a family doctor in Richmond, Virginia. "The pressure can damage your eardrums and hurt your Eustachian tubes." The Eustachian tube leads from the middle ear to the back of the nose and throat.

A SNEEZE CAN TRAVEL MORE THAN 100 MILES (161 KILOMETERS) PER HOUR. And the organs inside your skull (brain, eyes, eardrums, etc.) are tightly packed together. When you suppress a sneeze, the impact of the sneeze stays contained in your head. In rare cases, the force of that impact can cause serious damage.

A SNEEZE SENDS 2,000 TO 5,000 DROPLETS OF BACTERIA INTO THE AIR. So you should cover your nose and mouth when you sneeze, but . . .

YOUR HANDS ARE THE NUMBER-ONE WAY YOU CAN SPREAD BACTERIA, so it's better to sneeze into the crook of your bent arm.

IF YOU DO SNEEZE INTO YOUR HANDS, do everyone a favor and wash them thoroughly as soon as you can.

ACK! Acne!

There are a million great things about being a teenager. Acne isn't one of them. It is perfectly normal, though, and most teens have to deal with it to one degree or another.

Acne happens when **sebum** (an oily, sticky substance made in the skin) blocks your pores. Bacteria feed on the sebum, and that causes the pain,

swelling, and redness that comes with acne. Hormones and stress make acne worse—and that's why acne is so common among teens.

There are many different types of acne medication. Each attacks acne differently. Some dry the skin, some kill the bacteria that feed on the sebum, and some prevent your skin from making so much sebum. There are topical treatments, which are applied directly to your skin, and pills, which you take orally. Talk to your doctor about treatment. If your case is severe, you might be referred to a skin specialist, called a dermatologist. "I had a little bit of acne my freshman year," says Matthew M. "I went to a doctor, and now I take a pill for it every day. It's not that big a deal."

Here are some general health tips about acne:

DON'T PICK AT YOUR PIMPLES.
That will increase the inflammation and the chance of scars forming.

TRY TO KEEP YOUR HANDS AWAY FROM YOUR FACE. Your hands have oils and bacteria that can cause breakouts.

WASH YOUR FACE ONLY TWICE A DAY, and use an oil-free moisturizer. Many acne medicines dry the skin, and most soaps dry your skin even more.

IF POSSIBLE, TRY TO AVOID WORKING IN GREASY KITCHENS. The grease gets on your skin and can cause breakouts.

HAVE A HEALTHY OUTLET FOR STRESS because it can worsen acne. Whether it's exercise, music, meditation, or counseling— whatever helps you release tension will help your skin, too.

MOST IMPORTANT, DON'T GIVE UP! Stay patient and persistent, and you will definitely conquer your acne problem.

Sun Sense

The other thing you need to do to take care of your skin is to avoid getting sunburns or tans. "Just one blistering sunburn in childhood can double the risk of getting **melanoma** later in life," says Dr. Perry Robins, president of the Skin Cancer Foundation (SCF). Melanoma is the deadliest form of skin cancer.

A 2007 survey suggests that tanned skin might be losing popularity. Fifty-three percent of people surveyed by SCF and iVillage said that they don't look better with a tan.

But still, a lot of teens haven't gotten the message about the dangers of tanning. "I don't normally use sunscreen, because I have dark skin and I almost never burn," says Matthew M. "I got pretty lucky on that score." A tan's reputation as a "healthy glow" is bunk. A tan shows that your skin is already experiencing sun damage.

Nearly 2.3 million U.S. teenagers go to tanning beds each year. And again, this is a bad idea. According to SCF, research has found that the use of tanning beds during a person's teens and twenties can increase melanoma risk by 75 percent.

Luckily there are some pretty simple things you can do to protect your skin from the sun.

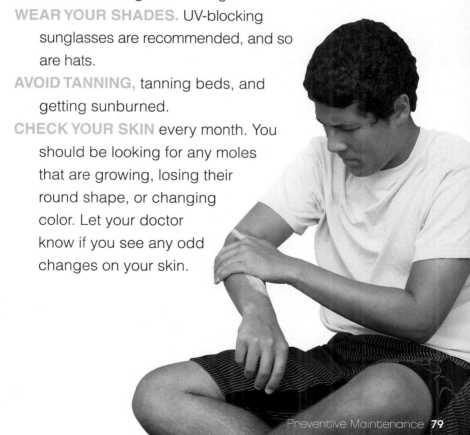

TRY TO CHILL IN THE SHADE during the middle of the day. The sun is strongest between 10 A.M. and 4 P.M.

USE A SUNSCREEN with an SPF of 15 or higher every day. Look for one that blocks both UVA and UVB rays of the sun.

USE A LOT OF SUNSCREEN—about 2 tablespoons. Apply it 30 minutes before going outside and again after two hours. Also reapply after swimming or sweating.

WEAR YOUR SHADES. UV-blocking sunglasses are recommended, and so are hats.

AVOID TANNING, tanning beds, and getting sunburned.

CHECK YOUR SKIN every month. You should be looking for any moles that are growing, losing their round shape, or changing color. Let your doctor know if you see any odd changes on your skin.

Smelling Smarts

On to a lighter, but smellier, topic: body odor. Like acne, this is one of those unpleasant things that everybody has to deal with to some degree. Why does it happen at all?

Sweating is part of your body's natural cooling system. When your body overheats, your brain sends a signal to your sweat glands—small, coiled organs found all over your skin. These glands begin to secrete salt, which draws water away from cells and blood in your body. The salt and the water then seep onto the surface of your skin and evaporate when exposed to the air. This evaporation causes your skin to cool down.

You may have noticed that sweat often smells. Smelly sweat is produced by special glands known as apocrine glands. When these glands secrete salt, they also shed some of their own cells, which then mix with the salt to produce protein and carbohydrates not found in regular sweat. When sweat from apocrine glands reaches your skin, it reacts with bacteria in the air and produces an odor in areas like your armpits and genitals.

So sweating is not only normal, it's necessary for your survival! But if you're concerned about the amount that you sweat, here's what you can do:

USE ANTIPERSPIRANT AND DEODORANT REGULARLY. Antiperspirants clog or reduce the size of pores so that less sweat can seep through them. Deodorants cover up or absorb bad smells without limiting sweat production. Your best bet is to use a product that is a combination of both.

USE BODY POWDER. It absorbs sweat like crazy and cools your skin. Look for one that is cornstarch based, instead of made from talc. Just make sure to put it on before you get dressed so you don't get powder all over your clothes.

TRY TO RELAX. This might be easier said than done, but taking deep breaths when you're nervous will allow more oxygen to flow through your body. As a result, you will feel more alert and less freaked out. The more relaxed you are, the less you'll perspire.

See your doctor if none of these suggestions work. You may have a condition that can be treated with a prescription antiperspirant/deodorant or by other methods.

BREATH
of Fresh Air

BAD BREATH is another one of those smells we all want to avoid. But scientists at King's College in London, England, may be on to something that could conquer even the worst breath. They have discovered that a type of bacteria already present in the human mouth works to freshen bad-breath odors. These researchers foresee a time when mouthwashes and toothpastes will contain chemicals that help these bacteria do their work and get rid of bad breath.

Until that day comes, there are things you can do to avoid getting bad breath. Brush your teeth—and your tongue—regularly. Floss at least once a day. Chewing gum can help and so can—believe it or not—chewing parsley. Avoid drinking coffee and, of course, don't smoke.

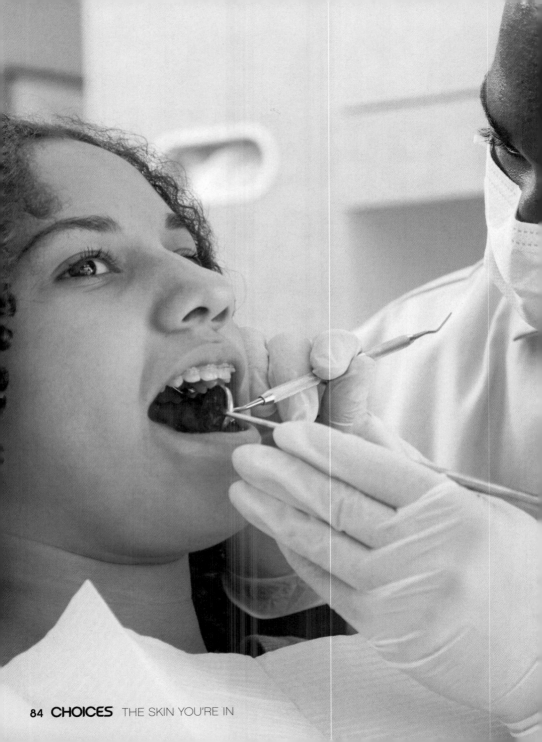

What's Up, Doc?

When was the last time you went to the doctor? How about the dentist? If you can't recall, it might be time to make an appointment. Teens should see their doctor and their dentist at least once a year.

Think of these professionals as your partners in taking care of yourself. You can talk to your doctor about any issues that might be bothering you. Don't be embarrassed—this person has a) lived through being a teenager and b) heard it all before. So don't be afraid to be honest!

Teens should see their doctor and their dentist at least once a year.

the big
pitfalls

the big pitfalls

AVOIDING THE MAJOR DANGERS OF TEEN LIFE

Safety First

Most of the things we have discussed so far in this book are changes that can maximize your health and well-being. Smart changes. Proactive changes. But not matters of life and death.

Now it's time to talk about matters of life and death.

Unfortunately, there are a few things you can do as a teen that are BIG MISTAKES. They are mistakes that are difficult, if not impossible, to recover from. Here's what you need to know about safe driving, alcohol abuse, and smoking.

A Lesson in Tragedy

Lydia wanted to be a fashion designer. Renee couldn't wait to go to Virginia Tech in the fall. Sarah was an athlete studying accounting at George Mason University. And Nettie was a French major, dreaming of studying at the Sorbonne in Paris one day.

But these four young lives were snuffed out in an instant, in a terrible car crash.

It happened on graduation night—June 15, 2007. Lydia Petkoff, Renee Shelkin, Sarah Carter, and Elaine "Nettie" Thackston were celebrating Lydia and Renee's graduation from West Potomac High School in Fairfax County, Virginia. A fifth teenager in the car escaped with minor injuries. Nettie, 20, was driving. She was a college student, and Sarah, 19, was her roommate. Sarah and Renee were cousins.

What happened? The girls were driving in a convertible on the huge six-lane Capital Beltway.

They were heading to a club in Washington, D.C. Nettie may have gotten confused about the exit she was supposed to take. Another car full of friends saw them turn onto an exit ramp and then swerve back into the path of a tractor-trailer truck.

Stephanie Talbot, 18, was driving the other car. "I was just thinking, 'Where are they going? What are they doing?'" she told the *Washington Post*. "I pulled over and I jumped over the barricade, and I just looked down." She saw her friends' bodies lying in the road. Stephanie called 911 on her cell phone and told her passengers not to get out of her car—"so they wouldn't see" what she'd seen, she said.

The 18-wheeler had smashed the car into the retaining wall and flipped it over. Three of the girls were thrown from the car. The car was demolished, and investigators couldn't tell for sure whether the convertible top had been up or down. They also couldn't immediately say whether the girls had been wearing their seat belts. There was alcohol in the car.

The Number-One Killer of Teens

These girls—and their families—did not deserve for this to happen. Nobody does. But the girls were doing a number of things that raised their risk of being involved in a fatal accident.

Car crashes are the biggest killer of people between the ages of 15 and 20. About 5,000 teens lose their lives each year in fatal accidents on U.S. roadways. Some of these accidents involve alcohol (about 17 percent), but most of them don't. What else causes deadly car accidents? Inexperienced

CAR
CRASHES
are the biggest killer of people between the ages of 15 and 20.

drivers, drowsy drivers, driving at night, and having the distraction of other kids in the car. Not using seat belts increases the odds of dying in accidents.

The girls from Virginia may not have realized all the chances they were taking. Driving at night, with five girls in one car, with alcohol in the car—these were all risks they didn't need to take. They could have gone to an all-night party their school was sponsoring at ESPN Zone. There was a bus to take teens to and from the party. Everyone who went to that party got home safely and lived to see another day.

Lydia, Renee, Sarah, and Nettie will never have another chance to make a better decision. But you do.

New Laws Save Lives

In the past ten years, most states have changed their laws about teen driving. After getting their learner's permits in these states, teens get a restricted license. The restrictions might limit nighttime driving or the number of teen passengers allowed in the car. The states with the most restrictive laws have seen crashes involving 16-year-old drivers decline by about 20 percent.

The states with the most restrictive laws have seen crashes involving 16-year-old drivers decline by about 20%.

20%

Whatever the laws of your state, here are simple things you can do to cut down your risk of a dangerous crash.

LOG 30 HOURS OF DRIVING with your mom, dad, or another experienced, licensed driver before you drive at night.

YOU SHOULD BE DRIVING FOR ABOUT SIX MONTHS before you carry other teen passengers.

DON'T DRIVE DROWSY. Get enough sleep to be sure this doesn't happen to you!

ALWAYS WEAR YOUR SEAT BELT and make sure all your passengers do, too. If you don't, you could get a ticket. More important, two-thirds of the people who die in car crashes were not wearing their seat belts.

NEVER DRINK AND DRIVE, and never get into a car with someone who has been drinking or doing drugs.

Underage Drinking

Another avoidable danger for teens is drinking. There are an estimated 11 million underage drinkers in the United States, and 7.2 million of them are binge drinkers, meaning they have five or more drinks in an evening. Why is this a big deal? "Too many Americans consider underage drinking a rite of passage to adulthood," says Dr. Kenneth Moritsugu, the former Acting U.S. Surgeon General.

"I've tasted alcohol, but I've never had a lot of it, and I've never been drunk," says Matthew M. of Louisiana. "I think it's unhealthy to make those kinds of decisions when you are young."

Matthew is right about that, and there are scientific studies that back him up. "Research shows that young people who start drinking before the age of 15 are five times more likely to have alcohol-related problems later in life," says Moritsugu. "New research also indicates that alcohol may harm the developing adolescent brain."

Alcohol-related problems can keep people from having good relationships. It can make it hard to keep a good job or do well in school. It can damage your judgment, your friendships, your health, and ultimately your life.

12 QUESTIONS About Alcohol and You

Is alcohol causing a problem in your life? If you answer yes to four or more of these 12 questions, you might have a problem with alcohol.

1. Do you drink because you have problems? To relax?
2. Do you drink when you get mad at other people, your friends or parents?
3. Do you prefer to drink alone, rather than with others?
4. Are your grades starting to slip? Are you goofing off on your job?
5. Did you ever try to stop drinking or drink less—and fail?
6. Have you begun to drink in the morning, before school or work?
7. Do you gulp your drinks?
8. Do you ever have loss of memory due to your drinking?
9. Do you lie about your drinking?
10. Do you ever get into trouble when you're drinking?
11. Do you get drunk when you drink, even when you don't mean to?
12. Do you think it's cool to be able to hold your liquor?

For more information on Alcoholics Anonymous, visit www.aa.org.

test
YOURSELF

What do you know about alcohol and peer pressure? You can test your knowledge of both at www.thecoolspot.gov. This site for teens is run by the National Institute on Alcohol Abuse and Alcoholism.

Teen Smoking

An estimated 800,000 teens tried smoking in 2006, which is good news for tobacco companies. Message to teen smokers: You've been played!

Most people don't start smoking late in life. The American Lung Association says 90 percent of regular smokers started smoking before they were 21. And then nicotine, the active ingredient in tobacco, gets its hooks into these young smokers.

"I have two cousins who smoke, and I think it's pretty ridiculous," says one teen. "I worked it out one day. If you spend $4 a day on cigarettes until you're 40, you're going down a very deep hole." How deep? If you buy cigarettes from ages 15 to 40, they'll cost you $36,500.

Nicotine is one of the most addictive substances on the planet. It is also one of the deadliest: 440,000 people die every year in the United States because of tobacco-related illnesses. Many people have lost a loved one to the diseases caused by cigarettes: lung cancer, heart attack, stroke, and emphysema.

But you have probably already heard this. Even though teens know the dangers, they start smoking because they think problems are a long way off. The truth is, though, nicotine starts hurting you right away. Sure, things like cancer are the long-term bad effects. But there are short-term bad effects, too.

YOUR LUNG CAPACITY GOES DOWN RIGHT AWAY. How cool is it to be 16 and sucking wind after you go up a flight of stairs? Not very.

YOUR BREATH, HAIR, HANDS, AND CLOTHES STINK TODAY—not years from now.

CIGARETTES PUT A DENT IN YOUR WALLET really quickly. Many cities are raising cigarette taxes to help pay for the medical expenses of people who have diseases caused by cigarettes.

Call It quits!

Mark Twain said, "Quitting smoking is easy. I've done it a thousand times." Smoking is just as addictive now as it was in Twain's day. But it *is* possible to quit. The latest research shows that a combination of counseling and medication may work best to help people quit smoking. If you want to quit, or someone you know wants to quit, start with a call to your doctor. He or she can probably connect you with a smoking cessation program in your community and may be able to prescribe medication that can increase your chances of quitting successfully.

The American Council on Science and Health maintains a Web site that explains everything a teen should know about tobacco.

"Everyone who has ever quit smoking will tell you that quitting is one of the toughest things they have ever done," ACSH reports. "The best way to avoid facing this tough problem, of course, is never to start smoking to begin with."

"The best way to avoid facing this tough problem . . . is never to start smoking to begin with."

FIND OUT
more!

To learn more about the effects of smoking and a million good reasons never to do it—or to quit if you've started—go to the Web site of the American Council on Science and Health:

thescooponsmoking.org

LIVING THE
GOODLIFE

HEY! WE'VE REACHED THE END OF THIS BOOK.

Hopefully, you've learned some things about how to take care of yourself and have fun doing so. Now it's time to put it all together. Some of the choices below are better than others. See how you do.

1 You just found out that your best friend has decided to go to the movies with somebody else. He didn't even call to see whether you were free first. How do you handle it?

a. Beat myself up. He's probably embarrassed to be seen with me.
b. Call somebody else and go out. We'll see each other soon.
c. Sit home alone eating a pint of ice cream.

2 Everyone's going out for pizza after the football game. You . . .
a. go, and have one cheese slice and some salad.
b. stay home, because you're trying to lose weight.
c. go, and eat three meat-lover's slices and a milk shake.

3 Which person got the right amount of exercise?

a. Person A: Walked between classes and spent the evening doing homework and watching TV.

b. Person B: Had a 30-minute jog before school, took the stairs between classes, and did some yoga stretches before bed.

c. Person C: Hit the gym after school and lifted weights for two hours.

4 You calculated your BMI and found out you need to be 10 pounds (5 kg) lighter to go from the overweight category to the normal category. What's the best strategy to get you there?

a. You go on a high-protein/low-carb diet.

b. You go on a high-carb/low-fat diet.

c. You start eating more fruits and vegetables, exercising almost every day, and keeping track of what you eat.

5 For maximum health, every night you should sleep for . . .

a. 9 hours.

b. 7 hours.

c. 5 hours.

6 Which factors can increase the risk of a teen car crash?

a. Having other teens in the car and being new behind the wheel.

b. Driving at night and being drowsy.

c. Both of the above.

Answer key: 1–b; 2–a; 3–b; 4–c; 5–a; 6–c

amino acids—the molecules that make up proteins

anorexia nervosa—a medical condition in which people deprive themselves of food

body mass index (BMI)—a ratio of height to weight; it is one way to compare healthy and unhealthy body weight

calories—units of energy; they provide a way to compare foods

cardiovascular—relating to the heart and blood vessels

dehydration—the state of being deprived of water; a dangerous health condition

diabetes—a disease in which the body loses the ability to process sugar in the bloodstream

epidemic—an outbreak of disease that affects a large number of individuals at the same time

fiber—a part of foods that passes through the digestive system without being digested; found in vegetables and whole grains

flexible—easily bendable; an important quality for joints and muscles

melanoma—the most dangerous form of skin cancer

micronutrients—nutrients the body needs in small quantities from food sources

obesity—a condition of being dangerously overweight

resistance training—weight-bearing exercises that build muscular strength

sebum—an oily, sticky substance produced by the skin, which can clog pores and cause acne

self-esteem—the regard one has for oneself

strenuous—difficult; requiring much energy

Books

Fletcher, Anne. *Weight Loss Confidential: How Teens Lose Weight and Keep It Off—and What They Wish Parents Knew*. Boston: Houghton Mifflin Company, 2006.

Heywood, Leslie. *Pretty Good for a Girl: An Athlete's Story*. Minneapolis: University of Minnesota Press, 2000.

Ingram, Scott. *Want Fries with That? Obesity and the Supersizing of America*. New York: Franklin Watts, 2005.

Jukes, Mavis. *The Guy Book: An Owner's Manual*. New York: Crown Publishers, 2002.

Jukes, Mavis, and Lilian Cheung. *Be Healthy! It's a Girl Thing: Food, Fitness, and Feeling Great*. New York: Crown, 2003.

Weiner, Jessica. *Do I Look Fat in This? Life Doesn't Begin Five Pounds from Now*. New York: Simon Spotlight Entertainment, 2006.

Weiner, Jessica. *A Very Hungry Girl: How I Filled Up on Life . . . and How You Can, Too!* Carlsbad, CA: Hay House, 2003.

Online Sites & Organizations

Action on Smoking and Health

www.ash.org
An antismoking and non-smokers' rights organization. Offers resources for information about smoking and health.

The Cool Spot

www.thecoolspot.gov
This site will help you separate fact from fiction on teens and drinking alcohol.

MyPyramid.gov—United States Department of Agriculture

www.mypyramid.gov
This site will give you a personalized eating and exercising strategy.

NIDA for Teens

teens.drugabuse.gov
NIDA—the National Institute on Drug Abuse—offers this science-based site for teens, with information, resources, facts and stats, and real-life stories about drug abuse.

The President's Challenge—Teens

www.presidentschallenge. org/home_teens.aspx
Learn about the President's Fitness Challenge and how you can participate. Includes tips on becoming more active.

Skin Cancer Foundation

www.skincancer.org
Everything you need to know about sun safety.

Students Against Destructive Decisions (SADD)

www.sadd.org
SADD is a teen leadership organization dedicated to preventing underage drinking, impaired driving, and other types of drug abuse.

TeensHealth

www.kidshealth.org/teen
Everything you need to know about keeping your mind and body healthy during your teen years.

Author's Note

Working on this book made me ask myself an important question: was I practicing what I preached? At first, the answer was a big fat NO!

But as I wrote, I realized that I needed to start exercising and keeping track of what I was eating again. I also needed to be kinder to myself. I joined a gym, and I actually did a lot of the reading I needed to do for research while jogging on an elliptical trainer. That felt good!

I can tell you from personal experience that exercising helps you sleep better at night. And better sleeping at night made concentrating on writing easier the next day. Give it a try!

This book relies on research and reporting that originally appeared in Scholastic *Choices* magazine. I want to acknowledge and thank my former colleague, editor Bob Hugel, and his able writers and reporters Denise Rinaldo, Libby Tucker, Marjorie Seidenfeld, Lynn Santa Lucia, Cara D'Amico, John DiConsiglio, Marisa Hoheb, Althea Zanecosky, Paul Hertel, Alan Roberts, and Janis Jibrin. If you liked this book, you'll love *Choices* magazine. Look for it in your library!

—Diane Webber